Advent:
The Journey to the Beginning

scripture, poetry, meditation, and prayer

Published by: Vers Chaotique LLC, Douglasville, Georgia, USA

Advent:
The Journey to the Beginning

scripture, poetry,
meditation,
and prayer

poetry by Kevin Schumaker
meditations and prayers by
Rev. Jamie Witt

For my daughter, Anna,

who always brings joy into my life, even during difficult and dark days. She reminds me that joy is always in front of me.

-   Reverend Jamie Witt

For my mother, who would have loved this book. And, for my father, who would not have understood why I wrote it, but would have been proud, nonetheless.

-   Kevin Schumaker

Table of Contents

i

Introduction by Kevin Schumaker:

The Enigma of Anticipation

I don't remember how old I was when Christmas changed for me. Memory can be like that sometimes. A memory sets itself in the landscape of your past in such a way that you know exactly what you saw and felt but have no idea when it happened. It can be seminal, formative, and as clear fifty-some years later, and yet you don't know precisely who you were when it happened. Perhaps that's because you were someone different after, and that prior person just ceased to be.

I do know this much. I was old enough not to believe in Santa Claus, exactly, but I didn't want to confess that I had lost such faith. There is that fuzzy time when you are between two states, a believer in magic, and knowing it's merely a trick. I suspect we have several of these in our lives. When we are moving from like to love, and sadly, on those occasions when we move back. The new you is still inchoate, but becoming them has already happened. It's a "both" time. And, it's a "neither" time.

Christmas was coming soon, and I was still young enough to want toys. My sister, two years older, had already moved on to wanting money, but she was always more mature than her age and practical beyond reason. I suspect the date was somewhere between Thanksgiving and the week of Christmas. This time, which is Advent for the Church, is a long and grueling period for a child, as they strive to be good so as not to tempt fate and risk missing out on a truly remarkable haul of gifts from Santa.

"There is no Santa," Lisa told me one afternoon when both parents were out and I was left in her care. "There is no Santa, and I can prove it." As stated, I'm not sure if I still fully believed in Santa at that time, but it did seem to be risking God's wrath to say such a thing out loud; it felt like the unforgivable sin of Christmas for every present-loving child.

I may have protested, or I may not have, but she led me to my parents' bedroom and opened their closet door. Now, to say my parents embraced a certain disorder in their bedroom would be polite. Inside the closet was a huge pile of clothes. Summer clothes, winter clothes, jackets that hadn't been worn in years, and slacks that still had the price tag still on them. A mountain of clothes. This, in itself, was not a surprise.

I'm not sure what I expected at that point, and my sister didn't give me long to contemplate the scene. Reaching in, she pulled back the top layer of clothes and revealed a pile of Christmas gifts. That they were my sister and my gifts from Santa was undeniable. My parents were always generous in that regard, and surveying that pile,

I say almost everything I'd asked for, and a few things I hadn't. In her final act of victory, my sister proclaimed, "No Santa."

As I stated, I don't know if I had any genuine belief in Santa before that moment. It was a subject I think I had kept preserved, fearful that if I gave it up, and the magic vanished, then so would all the joy of the holiday. In the end, that isn't what happened. Going forward, I continued to have wonderful and gift-rich holidays. But something did change. From then on, I no longer had the experience of true anticipation.

Christmas, for the child, is a time when they are filled with hope, but no guarantee. Thoughts of, "Have I been good enough? Will I get what I dream of? Will he come?" And, perhaps even more fundamentally, "How is any of this promise even possible?"

After the closet incident, I always knew that what was coming on Christmas day was already in the cards long before they were dealt. It was simply mechanical. By early December, the gifts I would get were already selected and purchased. Batteries were either bought or forgotten, and wrapping paper in plastic-covered rolls were hoarded next to a bag of tape and a box of bows that would never make it onto the gifts.

In other words, as Thanksgiving drew to a close, Christmas was already a done deal. There was no longer any hope to be felt. No fate yet to be decided. It was simply set. It was already all that it would ever be. All that was left was the ritual.

I think this is the problem we have with Christmas today. As Christians, we already know that the Christ child is going to be born that day. We know that his family would take him to the temple and eventually flee to Egypt. We know that after years, he will return, and that one day, as he approaches thirty, he will attend a wedding. We know that this wedding will be the beginning of his miracles and that they will continue with long walks, small and massive crowds. Three or so years will be filled with stories, friends, excitement, and disappointments. And, we know how it will end.

As Christians today, we all approach the holiday as children who have gazed into the closet and know the result. And thus, anticipation —the anticipation that contains both hope and fear, belief and doubt —has all collapsed. We simply stare and see how that day will unfold.

That is, of course, not how it was when we were children, and not how it would have been for those people longing for and dreaming of the coming of hope. The anticipation of what they hoped for, but were not confident would be—the anguish of aspiring to a dream.

In what follows, I do my best, as I walk through the Advent season, to try to go back to the time before the closet door opened. Through poetry, I try to touch on the feeling before the die is cast—the feeling of reaching out for the new day, uncertain that you will feel it. I will try to express the true, beautiful, and conflicted experience of anticipation that is Advent.

Kevin Schumaker

Introduction by Rev. Jamie Witt

Love in the Waiting

Christmas was magical for me because of my mom. She would start the season off on Thanksgiving night at dinner by putting George Winston's album *December* on the stereo. She would put it on repeat until the first of December and then she would add Tingstad and Rumble's *The Gift*. Then the closer it got to Christmas she would change it to one of Johnny Mathis' Christmas albums. It wasn't until I was a teenager that I learned that Johnny Mathis sang songs other than Christmas carols.

Music set the tone for me and then the lights followed quickly behind. The lights in the house were dimmed because of the Christmas tree lights. There was a soft glow about the house. The lights combined with the music became the magic of Christmas for me. I loved that time of year. To this day when I put on George Winston's *December* album I immediately feel a calm rush over me. My environment becomes peaceful. As a child I looked forward to that Christmas time so much because of the wonder and magic it held.

As an adult that magic started to fade. My mother got ill and changed. A friend once observed that Christmas was not near as magical as adults as it was as kids. I agreed. I now felt the stress and none of the magic. Problem was that I had a little girl now and it was my responsibility to make Christmas magic for her, the way my mom had for me.

I started playing music at Thanksgiving; George Winston's *December*, of course. I added to it Tingstand and Rumble's *The Gift.* And while we decorated the Christmas tree I played Johnny Mathis and Nat "King" Cole. I also dug out the old train set my parents had gotten me when I was 7 from a local store called "Tobins". It was an LGB train set made in "West Germany". I set it up and it ran beautifully and the memories began to flow. I remembered putting my pound puppies on the train for a ride and my She-ra dolls. My daughter also put pound puppies on the train and her Littlest Pet Shop toys. It was wonderful watching her enjoy the train and our Golden Retriever bark at it. With the light's dimmed and the music in the background the magic of Christmas was back for me.

I continued on to appreciate the anticipation of the Christmas season approaching. And not really the Christmas season, but the Advent season. The culmination of that season was Christmas but it was during Advent that all the magic happened. To this day I love the Advent season. A time of waiting and anticipation. A time of music and lights. A time waiting for the ultimate gift of love in the baby Jesus to arrive.

God gives us this entire season of waiting and anticipation to find the connections to family, friends, and love to find magic and lights. To find a way to let kindness into our hearts long enough to see the miracle of a Savior born to us. My prayer is that these Scripture readings, poems, meditations, and prayers carry you through the Advent season and help you experience anticipation, contemplation, wonder, light, joy, and love.

Rev. Jamie Witt

The Days that Precede the First Sunday

James 4:1-10

4 Those conflicts and disputes among you, where do they come from? Do they not come from your cravings that are at war within you? **2** You want something and do not have it, so you commit murder. And you covet something and cannot obtain it, so you engage in disputes and conflicts. You do not have because you do not ask. **3** You ask and do not receive because you ask wrongly, in order to spend what you get on your pleasures. **4** Adulterers! Do you not know that friendship with the world is enmity with God? Therefore whoever wishes to be a friend of the world becomes an enemy of God. **5** Or do you suppose that the scripture speaks to no purpose? Does the spirit that God caused to dwell in us desire envy? **6** But God gives all the more grace; therefore it says,
"God opposes the proud but gives grace to the humble."

7 Submit yourselves therefore to God. Resist the devil, and he will flee from you. **8** Draw near to God, and he will draw near to you. Cleanse your hands, you sinners, and purify your hearts, you double-minded. **9** Lament and mourn and weep. Let your laughter be turned into mourning and your joy into dejection. **10** Humble yourselves before the Lord, and he will exalt you.

Poem: Detente

Perhaps it is my eyes
that perceive the things of this world
filling me with anticipation of plenty

Perhaps it is the world
that seduces me with perfumes of pleasure
filling me with anticipation of joy

Perhaps it is you
that entices me with promises
filling me with anticipation of success

But I am never full
never getting satisfied
always longing
always hollow

The young prince from far away
Said craving is the problem
And now you say the same

So perhaps it is my hunger
set against my own heart
that brokers no detente

Perhaps it is my eyes
Perhaps it is the world
Perhaps it is you

Meditation:

Possessions and priorities are difficult to let go of in light of what we cannot see. God is asking to be first in our life. For us to trust God above our money, our possessions, our connections, our careers. We have faith...but do we really? Faith means blind trust in the One that holds all things together. An invisible force of love and goodness that holds us steady even though the boat dips and flows from side to side. That's life. Life is not steady, but the One who holds us is; yet we value other things above God. In freedom, let go! Let go of the place of supremacy that your material things hold. Let God move into that space. You need not get rid of your possessions and securities, just understand and honor the One who enables them to be yours and keep God first in your heart and in your priorities.

Prayer:

Gracious God, help me identify with the humble. Let me put aside my pride and possessions and realize that without You I would have none of those. For at my rock bottom none of those things were there, but You lifted me out of the darkness. **Amen**.

Hebrews 11:1-7

11 Now faith is the assurance of things hoped for, the conviction of things not seen. **2** Indeed, by faith our ancestors received approval. **3** By faith we understand that the worlds were prepared by the word of God, so that what is seen was made from things that are not visible.

The Examples of Abel, Enoch, and Noah

4 By faith Abel offered to God a more acceptable sacrifice than Cain's. Through this he received approval as righteous, God himself giving approval to his gifts; he died, but through his faith he still speaks. **5** By faith Enoch was taken so that he did not experience death, and "he was not found, because God had taken him." For it was attested before he was taken away that "he had pleased God." **6** And without faith it is impossible to please him, for whoever would approach God must believe that he exists and that he rewards those who seek him. **7** By faith Noah, warned by God about events as yet unseen, respected the warning and built an ark to save his household; by this he condemned the world and became an heir to the righteousness that is in accordance with faith.

POEM: The Gulf

The gulf that lies before us
home to all lose
and all hope
the wind whistles an ancient tune
of vertigo and sickness
yet I will leap
trusting the fall
and hum along with the song

Meditation:

By faith...by faith...by faith. The repetition of these two words is not accidental in the Hebrews text. Those that we look to in the Bible did not have certainty; they did not have assurance that nothing bad would happen to them as they followed God's path for them. In some cases they also had very little money or possessions. They had all that they needed though–they had faith and trust in God to guide and lead them. We like control and directions, facts and assurances. There are times when we have to let go of that need for control and lean more on our faith and trust in God. It is difficult to do, but very freeing. This Advent try to release control and walk by faith.

Prayer:

Lord God, we come to you knowing that we are stubborn about relinquishing control of our lives and what happens around us. In this busy season help us to slow down. Help us to align our thoughts and actions with Yours so that You may lead us with anticipation as we walk by faith with You. **Amen**.

Matthew 24:1-22

24 As Jesus came out of the temple and was going away, his disciples came to point out to him the buildings of the temple. **2** Then he asked them, "You see all these, do you not? Truly I tell you, not one stone will be left here upon another; all will be thrown down."

Signs of the End of the Age

3 When he was sitting on the Mount of Olives, the disciples came to him privately, saying, "Tell us, when will this be, and what will be the sign of your coming and of the end of the age?" **4** Jesus answered them, "Beware that no one leads you astray. **5** For many will come in my name, saying, 'I am the Messiah!' and they will lead many astray. **6** And you will hear of wars and rumors of wars; see that you are not alarmed, for this must take place, but the end is not yet. **7** For nation will rise against nation and kingdom against kingdom, and there will be famines and earthquakes in various places: **8** all this is but the beginning of the birth pangs.

Persecutions Foretold

9 "Then they will hand you over to be tortured and will put you to death, and you will be hated by all nations because of my name. **10** Then

13

many will fall away, and they will betray one another and hate one another. **11** And many false prophets will arise and lead many astray. **12** And because of the increase of lawlessness, the love of many will grow cold. **13** But the one who endures to the end will be saved. **14** And this good news of the kingdom will be proclaimed throughout the world, as a testimony to all the nations, and then the end will come.

The Desolating Sacrilege

15 "So when you see the desolating sacrilege, spoken of by the prophet Daniel, standing in the holy place (let the reader understand), **16** then those in Judea must flee to the mountains; **17** the one on the housetop must not go down to take things from the house; **18** the one in the field must not turn back to get a coat. **19** Woe to those who are pregnant and to those who are nursing infants in those days! **20** Pray that your flight may not be in winter or on a Sabbath. **21** For at that time there will be great suffering, such as has not been from the beginning of the world until now, no, and never will be. **22** And if those days had not been cut short, no one would be saved, but for the sake of the elect those days will be cut short.

POEM: **As You Leave**

As you leave
as you go away
I remind you of our home
of where we came together
and joined in love
in communion together

It'll fall as well
you promise me
as you walk away
leaving me to consider
the nature of love
and the nature of the coming storm

You'll fall again
you promise me
but beware of scoundrels who
promise you a wonderful life
and protection from the wars
that will batter me resolve

As you leave
I am unsettled
you always favor darker themes
expecting me to take comfort
in the shortness of the season
that will break us apart

Meditation:

Fear of what will be tends to haunt our thoughts as we approach the future. We want assurance and facts. We like to know what to expect and to know if any of our actions need to change in order to make the future better somehow. No matter the darkness; no matter the depth of worry you may find there is light to be found. There is the promise of Christ's constant presence with us. As we get tossed around and sometimes led astray Jesus is always coming to us and bearing the burdens with us. There is hope found in the destruction of things; it means there is something new waiting to be created. Life is a constant flow of death and resurrection; of fear and hope. Always hope and eternal new life.

Prayer:

Loving God, be close to us when we have fears about the future. Help us to remember that You go ahead of us into that unknown space and are ready to meet us there-no matter the situation. When something ends You always bring something new. Help me to see change this way. **Amen**.

Week 1: The First Steps

First Sunday of Advent
November 30, 2025

Matthew 24:36-44

36 "But about that day and hour no one knows, neither the angels of heaven, nor the Son, but only the Father. **37** For as the days of Noah were, so will be the coming of the Son of Man. **38** For as in the days before the flood they were eating and drinking, marrying and giving in marriage, until the day Noah entered the ark, **39** and they knew nothing until the flood came and swept them all away, so, too, will be the coming of the Son of Man. **40** Then two will be in the field; one will be taken, and one will be left. **41** Two women will be grinding meal together; one will be taken, and one will be left. **42** Keep awake, therefore, for you do not know on what day your Lord is coming. **43** But understand this: if the owner of the house had known in what part of the night the thief was coming, he would have stayed awake and would not have let his house be broken into. **44** Therefore you also must be ready, for the Son of Man is coming at an hour you do not expect.

Poem: *There is Another End*

There is another end
coming from so far away
that we misjudge the distance
like driving toward the mountains
that rise above a straight open plain
hour after hour ticking up
slightly higher, slightly taller
but never seeming to draw closer

and if I count the years
two by two they come
and load up all my hopes and fears
I still don't know when the tide will swell
to carry me away

There is this other end
an end that sits so far out
existing beyond our ability to see
that comes even after the end we anticipate
that comes even after the start we still await
the other further ending
that starts something newer
but we have to see through this start first

and if I count the years
two by two they come
and load up all my hopes and fears
I will not know the end of endings
until we start anew

Meditation:

There is comfort and peace to be found in resting into God's mysteries. There are things that our human brains are unable to handle or process. It doesn't stop us from asking the questions, but God knows we are not equipped for the answers. God knows the answers and God loves us. Resting into that truth and then allowing yourself to rest in the mystery of what we do not know but to know that God is handling it is a source of relief and comfort if you allow it to be. Life doesn't always makes sense, things aren't fair, and tragedy happens...but joy happens also. It's okay that we don't understand it all. We are held by the One who does.

Prayer:

Creator God, from the beginning of time You have known the workings of our world. You alone know your plan for redemption and resurrection. Help me to remember that it's not my business to try and control or worry about. Let me lean on my faith and trust in You and let go; allowing myself to rest in the mystery. **Amen**.

Hymn: "Awake! Awake, and Greet the New Morn" ELW 242

Romans 6:1-11

6 What then are we to say? Should we continue in sin in order that grace may increase? **2** By no means! How can we who died to sin go on living in it? **3** Do you not know that all of us who were baptized into Christ Jesus were baptized into his death? **4** Therefore we were buried with him by baptism into death, so that, just as Christ was raised from the dead by the glory of the Father, so we also might walk in newness of life.

5 For if we have been united with him in a death like his, we will certainly be united with him in a resurrection like his. **6** We know that our old self was crucified with him so that the body of sin might be destroyed, so we might no longer be enslaved to sin. **7** For whoever has died is freed[a] from sin. **8** But if we died with Christ, we believe that we will also live with him. **9** We know that Christ, being raised from the dead, will never die again; death no longer has dominion over him. **10** The death he died, he died to sin once for all, but the life he lives, he lives to God. **11** So you also must consider yourselves dead to sin and alive to God in Christ Jesus.

***Poem:* A Letter (#1)**

If I break myself again
will it please you
to be the one who saves me
I am willing to drink
and blind myself again
tearing myself apart

otherwise
I don't know
how to know
If you love me

Meditation:

John 1:16 tells us that through Jesus Christ we have all received grace upon grace. I love that verse...grace upon grace. This grace gives us freedom; not freedom to do and live however we like, but free from the bonds of sin and given the promise of eternal life. How we choose to use that freedom matters...not to our salvation because that has already been secured in the Cross. The freedom choice that matters is whether we joyfully accept the grace we have been given freely and then extend that grace to others or whether we ignore it and live however we please with no thought for those in need. God asks us to love our neighbors as we have been loved. We are called to live as Christ in the world around us, spreading love and grace around like confetti to brighten the gloom we so often encounter. Serve and live joyfully in the knowledge of grace and desire to share it.

Prayer:

Gracious God, we give you thanks for the abundant grace that You lavish upon us. Help us to share that grace with others and be Your hands and feet in the community we share. May

our response to Your love, be love to others.
Amen.

Hebrews 11:32-40

32 And what more should I say? For time would fail me to tell of Gideon, Barak, Samson, Jephthah, of David and Samuel and the prophets, **33** who through faith conquered kingdoms, administered justice, obtained promises, shut the mouths of lions, **34** quenched the power of fire, escaped the edge of the sword, were made strong out of weakness, became mighty in war, put foreign armies to flight. **35** Women received their dead by resurrection. Others were tortured, refusing to accept release, in order to obtain a better resurrection. **36** Others suffered mocking and flogging and even chains and imprisonment. **37** They were stoned to death; they were sawn in two; they were killed by the sword; they went about in skins of sheep and goats, destitute, persecuted, tormented— **38** of whom the world was not worthy. They wandered in deserts and mountains and in caves and holes in the ground.
39 Yet all these, though they were commended for their faith, did not receive what was promised, **40** since God had provided something better so that they would not, apart from us, be made perfect.

Poem: **A Letter (#2)**

I will offer a toast to my brothers
and sisters once burdened with shame
splintered from family and destitute
immolating their homes from within

I will offer a hug to my siblings
who once broken from a way that would heal
and crafted a community of exiles
and a path for me to follow through

this is
how I know
how I know
that you love me

Meditation:

The way is not always easy; in fact oftentimes the way of faith is the harder road to choose though it be the right one. During this Advent season there are moments of great anticipation that exudes excitement, but there are others experiencing moments of anticipation that bring sadness to the surface. For them it is an advent of loneliness and grief. Some churches hold Blue Christmas services to help those for whom the holidays are a difficult place to rest and worship God in this season in a different way—a way that honors their sadness. The Advent season reminds us of past Christmases as much as the anticipation of the one coming. When visiting old memories we think of those that have gone before us whom we now miss, but honor the way they paved a way of faith for us to follow.

Prayer:

Loving God, comfort those who mourn this Advent season. Help them to remember that You walk with them and hurt with them. We give thanks for the blessing of our loved one's lives and how they guided our faith and changed our lives. Be with those for whom this Advent is anticipation of sadness. **Amen**.

First Wednesday of Advent
December 3, 2025

Matthew 24:23-35

23 Then if anyone says to you, 'Look! Here is the Messiah!' or 'There he is!'—do not believe it. **24** For false messiahs and false prophets will appear and produce great signs and wonders, to lead astray, if possible, even the elect. **25** Take note, I have told you beforehand. **26** So, if they say to you, 'Look! He is in the wilderness,' do not go out. If they say, 'Look! He is in the inner rooms,' do not believe it. **27** For as the lightning comes from the east and flashes as far as the west, so will be the coming of the Son of Man. **28** Wherever the corpse is, there the eagles will gather.

The Coming of the Son of Man

29 "Immediately after the suffering of those days sun will be darkened, and the moon will not give its light; the stars will fall from heaven, and the powers of heaven will be shaken.

30 "Then the sign of the Son of Man will appear in heaven, and then all the tribes of the earth will mourn, and they will see 'the Son of Man coming on the clouds of heaven' with power and great glory. **31** And he will send out his angels with a loud trumpet call, and they will gather his elect from the four winds, from one end of heaven to the other.

The Lesson of the Fig Tree

32 "From the fig tree learn its lesson: as soon as its branch becomes tender and puts forth its leaves, you know that summer is near. **33** So also, when you see all these things, you know that he is near, at the very gates. **34** Truly I tell you, this generation will not pass away until all these things have taken place. **35** Heaven and earth will pass away, but my words will not pass away.

***Poem:* how it'll end**

Shall I tell you then, how it'll end
and be like the carnival barkers
or snake oil salesmen on the road
the men in fine suits that proclaim the coming
day

I could suggest where to travel
imply that you race on
to inquire with high beam eyes
and a hunger for the denouement

Because we are creatures of the end
finish lines and checkered flags
tearful eulogies so well written
the end game and the final tally done

Shall I tell you, then, how it will end
because we abjore the anticipation
always cut to the chase
we eschew living toward what we don't yet have

Meditation:

I have a friend who hates to go on rollercoasters that go backward and he can't see what's up ahead of him. He said it is so unsettling to be riding along and not having a clue what is coming next. I think that is pretty natural. In Scripture the disciples are always questioning Jesus about what will indicate the end times. They want an itemized list so they know what to expect. They don't want to be on that ride backwards. I think we are all like that. We like to know what to expect and we like solid answers to our questions. This is another mystery that God asks that we have faith and trust in Him to handle. God knows and God loves us so we can rest in that mystery too with peaceful anticipation.

Prayer:

Faithful God, You love us and hold us through our constant questioning and doubt. Help us to rest in the knowledge that we can rest in the mystery as You dwell in the truth. Let the ability to let go of the need for answers help to lighten our load. **Amen**.

Hymn: "Soon and Very Soon" ELW 439

Acts 1:12-17, 21-26

12 Then they returned to Jerusalem from the mount called Olivet, which is near Jerusalem, a Sabbath day's journey away. **13** When they had entered the city, they went to the room upstairs where they were staying: Peter, and John, and James, and Andrew, Philip and Thomas, Bartholomew and Matthew, James son of Alphaeus, and Simon the Zealot, and Judas son of James. **14** All these were constantly devoting themselves to prayer, together with certain women, including Mary the mother of Jesus, as well as his brothers.

15 In those days Peter stood up among the brothers and sisters (together the crowd numbered about one hundred twenty persons) and said, **16** "Brothers and sisters, the scripture had to be fulfilled, which the Holy Spirit through David foretold concerning Judas, who became a guide for those who arrested Jesus, **17** for he was numbered among us and was allotted his share in this ministry."

21 "So one of the men who have accompanied us during all the time that the Lord Jesus went in and out among us, **22** beginning from the baptism of John until the day when he was taken up from us—one of these must become a witness with us to his resurrection." **23** So they proposed two, Joseph called Barsabbas, who was also known as Justus, and Matthias. **24** Then they prayed and said, "Lord, you know everyone's heart. Show us which one of these two you have chosen **25** to take the place in this ministry and apostleship from which Judas turned aside to go to his own place." **26** And they cast lots for them, and the lot fell on Matthias, and he was added to the eleven apostles.

Poem: **The Luck of the Draw**

Even when I win I am forgotten
I was not picked
not selected
not singled out
and invited in
like the glorious ones
hand-picked to be beloved
or taken to mountaintops
to behold some greater truth

An afterthought, perhaps
a fifty-fifty shot
of even being seen
and with many names
It's still just the luck of the draw
that I was here
when the need to fill a hole arose
nearly an error
because even when I win I am forgotten

Meditation:

It is sometimes difficult to see where the contributions of one person can make a significant difference in a hurting world. It can be discouraging and sometimes lead to someone not doing anything at all out of a feeling of futility. God created each one of us and brought us into the world in the same way Jesus was–as a baby to learn and grow. We were also each born with special gifts and abilities. We are called to use those gifts to make our small corner of the world a better place. Keep doing what you can; keep loving; keep serving. It may feel that our small contributions will be forgotten but the love and kindness we share in God's name is never forgotten for the person who desperately needed it.

Prayer:

God of love, when it feels that our good works are not enough to express the joy of receiving your grace, give us the endurance to do them anyway. Remind us that we each have a place, a time, and a gift to share. Inspire our work and desire to live out the Gospel. **Amen**.

Matthew 13:16-25

16 "But blessed are your eyes, for they see, and your ears, for they hear. **17** Truly I tell you, many prophets and righteous people longed to see what you see but did not see it and to hear what you hear but did not hear it.

The Parable of the Sower Explained

18 "Hear, then, the parable of the sower. **19** When anyone hears the word of the kingdom and does not understand it, the evil one comes and snatches away what is sown in the heart; this is what was sown on the path. **20** As for what was sown on rocky ground, this is the one who hears the word and immediately receives it with joy, **21** yet such a person has no root but endures only for a while, and when trouble or persecution arises on account of the word, that person immediately falls away. **22** As for what was sown among thorns, this is the one who hears the word, but the cares of this age and the lure of wealth choke the word, and it yields nothing. **23** But as for what was sown on good soil, this is the one who hears the word and understands it, who indeed bears fruit and yields in one case a hundredfold, in another sixty, and in another thirty."

The Parable of Weeds among the Wheat

24 He put before them another parable: "The kingdom of heaven may be compared to someone who sowed good seed in his field, **25** but while everybody was asleep an enemy came and sowed weeds among the wheat and then went away.

Poem: To sit

To sit among the weeds
and open your lungs
and breathe in the smell of earth
damp but rich with leaves decomposing
is to sit in a place of hope

To sit among the weeds
and open your ears
and catch the sound of a limb falling
from a tree far off, past its prime
is to sit in a place of history

To sit among the weeds
and open your hands
and feel the sun warming
changing overnight dew to vapor
is to sit in a place of beginning

To sit among the weeds
and open your eyes
and see only flowers and leaves
the mad rush of insects
is to sit in the kingdom of heaven

Meditation:

I used to pick giant bouquets of dandelions when I was a child to present to my mom. To me, they were flowers, not weeds, and they were beautiful. We live in a world where we try our best to tend to God's Word and embrace it in the way we interact with each other. Even when we do all the right things there are times that we experience difficulties. There is sin in this world and there are times that it can feel like an enemy coming and bringing you challenges. Remember that God's kingdom is here and not yet. We dwell in the kingdom now and Jesus bears all things with us. When difficulties and challenges have come my way I have often found that I experienced more growth and a stronger faith from going through them. In fact, I wouldn't be who I am today without the weeds I had to work with and around. God took those weeds and used them for my good–helping me grow in strength and knowledge. So, for me weeds are not always ugly. They can be dandelions after a touch from God.

Prayer:

Lord God, may we turn to You when troubles arise to help us find a blessing in the struggle.

May we remember that following You doesn't guarantee freedom from all misfortunes; but it does guarantee us a loving companion through them. Thank you for your ability to comfort and guide me. **Amen**.

John 1:19-28

19 This is the testimony given by John when the Jews sent priests and Levites from Jerusalem to ask him, "Who are you?" **20** He confessed and did not deny it, but he confessed, "I am not the Messiah." **21** And they asked him, "What then? Are you Elijah?" He said, "I am not." "Are you the prophet?" He answered, "No." **22** Then they said to him, "Who are you? Let us have an answer for those who sent us. What do you say about yourself?" **23** He said,

"I am the voice of one crying out in the wilderness, 'Make straight the way of the Lord,'" as the prophet Isaiah said.

24 Now they had been sent from the Pharisees. **25** They asked him, "Why, then, are you baptizing if you are neither the Messiah, nor Elijah, nor the prophet?" **26** John answered them, "I baptize with water. Among you stands one whom you do not know, **27** the one who is coming after me; I am not worthy to untie the strap of his sandal." **28** This took place in Bethany across the Jordan where John was baptizing.

***Poem:* I'd rather**

I'd rather be John

than any other

and cry out

from the wood

than to be expected

to heed the call

Meditation:

John the Baptist is an interesting character and we get to hear him a lot during the Advent season. He announces the arrival of the Messiah, which is something we anticipate during this Advent season. What we also continue to anticipate is the time when Christ will come again. The Advent of Jesus as a baby reminds us to look for Him again in an age yet to come. John's strength of faith and complete trust in God is enviable. John calls to those around him to change their ways and be baptized because the Messiah is coming soon. Responding and accepting a call that changes your life is not an easy task. I am proud and in awe of those around John at the time that answered yes to that call and then committed themselves to a new way of grace filled love in their lives. We are all still called. How do you respond?

Prayer:

Great and glorious God, You call us to follow You, to follow the way of love and grace even when it runs contrary to our society's norms. Help us to have the courage to embrace Your will and way for us even when it is difficult. **Amen**.

Week 2: The Call

Second Sunday of Advent
December 7, 2025

Matthew 3:1-12

1 In those days John the Baptist appeared in the wilderness of Judea, proclaiming, **2** "Repent, for the kingdom of heaven has come near.", **3** This is the one of whom the prophet Isaiah spoke when he said, "The voice of one crying out in the wilderness: 'Prepare the way of the Lord; make his paths straight.' " **4** Now John wore clothing of camel's hair with a leather belt around his waist, and his food was locusts and wild honey. **5** Then Jerusalem and all Judea and all the region around the Jordan were going out to him, **6** and they were baptized by him in the River Jordan, confessing their sins. **7** But when he saw many of the Pharisees and Sadducees coming for his baptism, he said to them, "You brood of vipers! Who warned you to flee from the coming wrath? **8** Therefore, bear fruit worthy of repentance, **9** and do not presume to say to yourselves, 'We have Abraham as our ancestor,' for I tell you, God is able from these stones to raise up children to Abraham. **10** Even now the ax is lying at the root of the trees; therefore every tree that does not bear good fruit will be cut down and thrown into the fire. **11** "I baptize you with water for repentance, but the one who is coming after me is more powerful than I, and I am not worthy to carry his sandals. He will baptize you with the Holy Spirit and fire. **12** His winnowing fork is in his hand, and he will clear his threshing floor and will gather his wheat into the granary, but the chaff he will burn with unquenchable fire."

Poem: A Cardboard Sign

The world drowns me in crying
broken bits of this and that
exclamations, derogations, things I might have
done
and recommendations for new shoes and drugs

So I apply my millionaire mindset
unfurl my my high performance way
recite my daily affirmations
to keep me safe on the road ahead

To find a single voice
in this forest of trees
I confess when I lay down to sleep
feels like too great a task

I know to avoid the vipers
cautions are the currency of these times
warnings about investments
and fluoride in the water

So I block out the distractions
to emerge each day anew
girded for each battle
and permit no detour from my way

To find a single voice
in this forest of trees
I confess when I lay down to sleep
feels like too great a task

The world drowns me in buying
shiny bits of this and that
vacations, separations, things I might still do
and a sudden breakthrough in the world of drugs

The man stands on the off-ramp
matted beard and styrofoam cup
a cardboard sign for donations
saying "God bless you for the help"

Meditation:

This story is a struggle for us to hear, especially around this time of year. It makes me wonder about the motives of the Pharisees and Sadducees in seeking out to be baptized by John. Perhaps it was a selfish desire to seek forgiveness for things they would continue to do again; or maybe did some of them want to break away and start a new life? I don't like to assume other people's motives without hearing their story. Even if John's words are harsh, maybe they had a cleansing effect on those assembled for the wrong reasons. That's my hope anyway. This is a good time for all of us to reexamine our hearts, motives, and priorities in our walk with Christ. During Advent we tend to be kinder people as the joy of Christmas approaches. I've often thought the world would be a better place if we could keep that Christmas mindset all year long...that by July we didn't need a good "brood of vipers" lecture to get us back to our faith. This year try to hold on to that December feeling for the whole year. Perhaps keep a nativity scene out all year long to remind you. As we celebrate with joy in our faith as Christmas approaches we must try to continue to celebrate this way with joy as we await Christ's return again.

Prayer:

Lord God, hold our hearts in this season of love and joy. Help us to keep the love for You and neighbor close all year long. May our faith in You and need for grace always be our mindset. **Amen**.

Hymn: "On Jordan's Bank the Baptist's Cry" ELW 249

1 Thessalonians 4:1-12

4 Finally, brothers and sisters, we ask and urge you in the Lord Jesus that, as you learned from us how you ought to live and to please God (as, in fact, you are doing), you should do so more and more. **2** For you know what instructions we gave you through the Lord Jesus. **3** For this is the will of God, your sanctification: that you abstain from sexual immorality; **4** that each one of you know how to control your own body in holiness and honor, **5** not with lustful passion, like the gentiles who do not know God; **6** that no one wrong or exploit a brother or sister in this matter, because the Lord is an avenger in all these things, just as we have already told you beforehand and solemnly warned you. **7** For God did not call us to impurity but in holiness. **8** Therefore whoever rejects this rejects not human authority but God, who also gives his Holy Spirit to you.
9 Now concerning love of the brothers and sisters, you do not need to have anyone write to you, for you yourselves have been taught by God to love one another, **10** and indeed you do love all the brothers and sisters throughout Macedonia. But we urge you, brothers and sisters, to do so more and more, **11** to aspire to live quietly, to mind your own affairs, and to work with your hands, as we directed you, **12** so that

you may behave properly toward outsiders and be dependent on no one.

Poem: **The Letter (#3)**

The doctor wrote me a letter
in the form of a prescription
for a drug I already had
"Remember to take it," she said and added
"Just like you already know how to do."

But the drug can be such a bother
I am only hurting myself
and certainly not any others
that get in my way
and thus
get only what I decide they need

Meditation:

Just like the Thessalonians we sometimes need a gentle reminder to love one another. It sounds so simple, but anyone who has tried to respect, care about, and pray for someone that we don't like or who has hurt us in some way knows how difficult this command from Jesus truly is. It may be the hardest thing we are called to do as Christians, which is why we all need a reminder now and again. Loving one's neighbors means **all** our neighbors; the ones we love naturally and the ones we struggle with; the ones who live far away and maybe worship differently; the ones who use their words to hurt. During the holiday season it seems easier in some ways to put aside our grievances with one another than during the rest of the year. Jesus called loving God and loving neighbor the greatest commandment and it is; but it is also the hardest.

Prayer:

Loving God, help us to be a people that defaults to love in difficult situations. Guide us to follow the mind of Christ and offer forgiveness and grace. We thank you for Your grace with us when we fail to find love to give. Continually work in us and through us the whole of our lives. **Amen**.

Romans 15:14-21

14 I myself feel confident about you, my brothers and sisters, that you yourselves are full of goodness, filled with all knowledge, and able to instruct one another. **15** Nevertheless, on some points I have written to you rather boldly by way of reminder, because of the grace given me by God **16** to be a minister of Christ Jesus to the gentiles in the priestly service of the Gospel of God, so that the offering of the gentiles may be acceptable, sanctified by the Holy Spirit. **17** In Christ Jesus, then, I have reason to boast of my work for God. **18** For I will not be so bold as to speak of anything except what Christ has accomplished through me to win obedience from the gentiles, by word and deed, **19** by the power of signs and wonders, by the power of the Spirit, so that from Jerusalem and as far around as Illyricum I have fully proclaimed the Gospel of Christ. **20** Thus I make it my ambition to proclaim the Gospel, not where Christ has already been named, so that I do not build on someone else's foundation, **21** but as it is written,

"Those who have never been told of him shall see, and those who have never heard of him shall understand."

Poem: **The Letter (#4)**

My mailbox is choking with adverts
solicitations, enticements, endorsements
from people that know better than I
so, I toss them in the recycle bin
knowing that I'll see them again

Meditation:

Today would have been my mom's 76th birthday. Unfortunately, she passed away 10 years ago but when I was a child my mom helped nurture my faith by telling me about Jesus, teaching me prayers, and showing me how to be Jesus in the world around me. She loved serving others but did not like getting credit for it. One time a close friend of mine wanted to go to a winter church camp, but couldn't afford the cost. She lived with her single mom and sister and money was tight. My mom contacted the church and anonymously paid for her to go to camp. This is just one of the ways my mom worked behind the scenes as the hands and feet of Christ. Perhaps she should have boasted more, like Paul, but she just wanted to spread kindness in a quiet way; in her own way.

Prayer:

Lord God, guide us toward opportunities to be Your hands and feet in this hurting world. May we spread love and kindness to those who desperately need it. May they know You through us. **Amen**.

Second Wednesday of Advent
December 10, 2025

Matthew 12:33-37

33 "Either make the tree good and its fruit good, or make the tree bad and its fruit bad, for the tree is known by its fruit. **34** You brood of vipers! How can you speak good things when you are evil? For out of the abundance of the heart the mouth speaks. **35** The good person brings good things out of a good treasure, and the evil person brings evil things out of an evil treasure. **36** I tell you, on the day of judgment you will have to give an account for every careless word you utter, **37** for by your words you will be justified, and by your words you will be condemned."

Poem: **Such a Scandalous Thing**

Forgive me please
for I misspoke
I'm not sure where that came from
precision is such a scandalous thing
so don't ignore my intention

I promise you my words
are misconstrued by you
my brethren

I'd go so far
as to suggest
you substituted your own intention

No, no, misread me not
I shouldn't say
My words' heart is simply flawless

But I promise you
I give you my word
my language is well-intentioned

Judge me not
by that off-hand slur
and insulting impression

Though I will suggest
you were the first
to question my suggestion

Render a verdict only

on what I say
what is in my heart of gold

and not in the way
I speak so freely
when I suspect you would agree

I can't have you
out there spreading lies
based solely on my own words

There is no accounting
for my professions
I don't know where they come from

Meditation:

Sticks and stones…the rhyme we all learned but sadly it's a lie. Words can hurt us more than physical pain at times. In today's world words can fly on social media and insults can be made without even having to be face to face with someone. This causes words to be even more hurtful as some forget there is a real person reading those words on the other side of the screen. Ephesians 4:29 says, "Let no evil talk come out of your mouths, but only what is useful for building up, as there is need, so that your words may give grace to those who hear." In the Gospel according to Matthew 15:11, Jesus says, "…it is not what goes into the mouth that defiles a person, but it is what comes out of the mouth that defiles." Clearly sharp cutting words is nothing new in our society. As Christians we follow Jesus and His teachings. Even though it can be difficult at times, we need to not let heightened emotions control our words. A careless word can never be unsaid. Let us speak grace to build one another up as we journey together in faith.

Prayer:

Dearest Christ Jesus, there are times where Your command to love our neighbor is so difficult. Please help me consider my words before I speak and use them carefully. May the words that come from my mouth communicate grace and Your love. **Amen**.

Hymn: "Lord, Speak to Us, That We May Speak" ELW 676

2 Peter 3:1-10

3 This is now, beloved, the second letter I am writing to you; in them I am trying to arouse your sincere intention by reminding you **2** that you should remember the words spoken in the past by the holy prophets and the commandment of the Lord and Savior spoken through your apostles. **3** First of all you must understand this, that in the last days scoffers will come, scoffing and indulging their own lusts **4** and saying, "Where is the promise of his coming? For ever since our ancestors died, all things continue as they were from the beginning of creation!" **5** They deliberately ignore this fact, that by the word of God heavens existed long ago and an earth was formed out of water and by means of water, **6** through which the world of that time was deluged with water and perished. **7** But by the same word the present heavens and earth have been reserved for fire, being kept until the day of judgment and destruction of the godless. **8** But do not ignore this one fact, beloved, that with the Lord one day is like a thousand years, and a thousand years are like one day. **9** The Lord is not slow about his promise, as some think of slowness, but is patient with you, not wanting any to perish but all to come to repentance. **10** But the day of the Lord will come like a thief, and then the heavens will pass away with a loud noise, and the elements will be destroyed with fire, and the earth and everything that is done on it will be disclosed.

Poem: The Letter (#5)

I call you beloved
begging you to wait
as days and years
feel so long
and we are tempted
by the rallies and cries
of those who mock our bidding

We are so narrow
we are so small
as days and years
feel so long
and we hunger
for certainty
promises of certainty

I call you beloved
seeking your return
as days and years
feel so long
the blessings foretold
still loom, I do assure

Meditation:

"...that with the Lord one day is like a thousand years, and a thousand years are like one day." As humans we like chronos time; we like things happening chronologically and the clock ticking the hours, minutes, and seconds of the day away; until a new day begins and the cycle starts all over. God runs on kairos time which is hard for us to conceptualize. Kairos time happens when we share a moment with God that creates a significant experience for us. God determines the time. God hears all our prayers and God keeps His promises, but on God's time. We often think that God hasn't heard or answered our prayers; God seems silent. God hears and responds on kairos time and sometimes not in the way we want. Many times what we want is not what we need; and like a petulant child we turn on God in our anger and claim our prayer wasn't answered. Prayer requires patience and trust in God, who truly does know what we need better than we do. This advent slow down, enjoy every moment, not worried about the clock, but about the heart.

Prayer:

Eternal God, forgive us our impatience and often inability to consider time in the way You do. Please continue to work with us, in us, and through us to keep us safe from our own selfish wants and to turn to You to know our needs. **Amen**.

2 Peter 3:11-18

11 Since all these things are to be destroyed in this way, what sort of persons ought you to be in leading lives of holiness and godliness, **12** waiting for and hastening the coming of the day of God, because of which the heavens will be set ablaze and destroyed and the elements will melt with fire? **13** But, in accordance with his promise, we wait for new heavens and a new earth, where righteousness is at home.

Final Exhortation and Doxology

14 Therefore, beloved, while you are waiting for these things, strive to be found by him at peace, without spot or blemish, **15** and regard the patience of our Lord as salvation. So also our beloved brother Paul wrote to you according to the wisdom given him, **16** speaking of this as he does in all his letters. There are some things in them hard to understand, which the ignorant and unstable twist to their own destruction, as they do the other scriptures. **17** You therefore, beloved, since you are forewarned, beware that you are not carried away with the error of the lawless and lose your own stability. **18** But grow in the grace and knowledge of our Lord and Savior Jesus Christ. To him be the glory both now and to the day of eternity. Amen.

Poem: **The Letter (#6)**

When you left I saw no stain
no mark of errors you made here
    all the slights
    all the ill-timed words
    all tones too harsh

I think you left me correctly
although it came as a surprise
    it always does
    the scaffolding falls
    and you vanished through the floor

Living is a high-wire act
high-voltage in the rain
    you bore it as well as you could
    the imperfections so capturing
    the grace of the day

Meditation:

I love the look in someone's eyes nearing the end of their long life when they say they have no regrets. Is that what being found by God in peace is like? A patient in the hospital once told me that we all make mistakes but we don't all learn from them. If we learn something then we should give ourselves grace and then keep going cherishing our newly found wisdom. Perhaps that is how we can be found in peace and also grow in grace. We make so many choices as our lives journey forward–some good, some not so good. No matter how we choose, God is with us to comfort and wrap in grace what hurts when we make a mistake and look for a way to interject a blessing and also there when life seems to flow peacefully along. God is in it with us during peace and during challenges. Through it all may we continue to "grow in the grace and knowledge of our Lord and Savior Jesus Christ."

Prayer:

Lord God, may we feel Your peace with us as we journey through life and help us to share that peace with others. **Amen**.

Luke 3:1-18

3 In the fifteenth year of the reign of Tiberius Caesar, when Pontius Pilate was governor of Judea, and Herod was ruler of Galilee, and his brother Philip ruler of the region of Ituraea and Trachonitis, and Lysanias ruler of Abilene, **2** during the high priesthood of Annas and Caiaphas, the word of God came to John son of Zechariah in the wilderness. **3** He went into all the region around the Jordan, proclaiming a baptism of repentance for the forgiveness of sins, **4** as it is written in the book of the words of the prophet Isaiah,

"The voice of one crying out in the wilderness: 'Prepare the way of the Lord; make his paths straight.

5 Every valley shall be filled, and every mountain and hill shall be made low, and the crooked shall be made straight, and the rough ways made smooth,

6 and all flesh shall see the salvation of God.' "

7 John said to the crowds coming out to be baptized by him, "You brood of vipers! Who warned you to flee from the coming wrath? **8** Therefore, bear fruits worthy of repentance, and do not begin to say to yourselves, 'We have

Abraham as our ancestor,' for I tell you, God is able from these stones to raise up children to Abraham. **9** Even now the ax is lying at the root of the trees; therefore every tree that does not bear good fruit will be cut down and thrown into the fire."

10 And the crowds asked him, "What, then, should we do?" **11** In reply he said to them, "Whoever has two coats must share with anyone who has none, and whoever has food must do likewise." **12** Even tax collectors came to be baptized, and they asked him, "Teacher, what should we do?" **13** He said to them, "Collect no more than the amount prescribed for you." **14** Soldiers also asked him, "And we, what should we do?" He said to them, "Do not extort money from anyone by threats or false accusation, and be satisfied with your wages."

15 As the people were filled with expectation and all were questioning in their hearts concerning John, whether he might be the Messiah, **16** John answered all of them by saying, "I baptize you with water, but one who is more powerful than I is coming; I am not worthy to untie the strap of his sandals. He will baptize you with the Holy Spirit and fire. **17** His winnowing fork is in his hand to clear his threshing floor and to gather the wheat into his granary, but the chaff he will burn with unquenchable fire."

18 So with many other exhortations he proclaimed the good news to the people.

Poem: **And so...**

And so it begins
I tell you
but be forewarned
the message tomorrow
is not really so different
from what it was before

The child does not grow less hungry
only after you call him to dinner
and the storm doesn't drench her
only after you clothe her
so in anticipation of tomorrow I ask
What   besides   the   exhortations   will   be
unchanged?

Meditation:

"What shall we do?" Each group asks John the same question and his response guides them to live their lives loving their neighbors. Look at each question and response. If the people just loved/respected the people around them then the question of what to do wouldn't even need to be asked. As Lutherans we are called to respond with joy to the grace we have received from God and in that joy is serving God and each other. The grace and love we share with others doesn't earn us salvation, Jesus already did that for us on the Cross. Salvation is secured; rest in the joy of that grace and then take that feeling out into the world around you to create more joy. And if you're ever unsure of the right move, just remember the people asking John, "What shall we do?" and his answer. Paired with Christ's love that should guide you.

Prayer:

Gracious God, help us to remember the meaning of your servant John's words and live our lives honestly, fairly, and with grace extended to our neighbors. May You be ever closer to us when we are tempted or when our neighbor is difficult. Guide to always choose grace. **Amen**.

Week 3: Well Met

Third Sunday of Advent
December 14, 2025

Matthew 11:2-11

2 When John heard in prison what the Messiah was doing, he sent word by his disciples **3** and said to him, "Are you the one who is to come, or are we to wait for another?" **4** Jesus answered them, "Go and tell John what you hear and see: **5** the blind receive their sight, the lame walk, those with a skin disease are cleansed, the deaf hear, the dead are raised, and the poor have good news brought to them. **6** And blessed is anyone who takes no offense at me."

Jesus Praises John the Baptist

7 As they went away, Jesus began to speak to the crowds about John: "What did you go out into the wilderness to look at? A reed shaken by the wind? **8** What, then, did you go out to see? Someone dressed in soft robes? Look, those who wear soft robes are in royal palaces. **9** What, then, did you go out to see? A prophet? Yes, I tell you, and more than a prophet. **10** This is the one about whom it is written,

'See, I am sending my messenger ahead of you, who will prepare your way before you.'

11 "Truly I tell you, among those born of women no one has arisen greater than John the Baptist, yet the least in the kingdom of heaven is greater than he.

Poem: **The Enigma of My Crime**

I'll be content to wait
if that is the sentence I face
to live in anticipation
the enigma of my crime

Though one last inquiry
if it reaches your ears
will mean it wasn't in vain
was this ever your way

Was I in my way the prophet
for this age or the next
or did I escape a palace
for just a dirty cell

I'll be content to wait
if that is the sentence I face
to live in anticipation
the enigma of my crime

I answered the call I heard
and yelled across the land
I accepted what the world provided
the sweetness of it all

I offended and I swore
and took pleasure in their stares
an indulgence I allowed myself
more comforting than silken robes

I'll be content to wait

if that is the sentence I face
to live in anticipation
the enigma of my crime

I was born my mothers' child
and I committed to her oath
and I accept your final verdict
that the saints are greater then me

the enigma of my time

Meditation:

Obviously Jesus loved John the Baptist dearly and held him in high esteem for his role as a prophet among the people and the herald of His coming. He praises John to the crowd that assembles and points to John's call as a herald of the Messiah's coming. At the end of his praise though he says, "yet the least in the Kingdom of heaven in greater that he [John]." Just as in Jesus' time we live in a hierarchical society where people are categorized by their importance or lack of. Jesus is trying to tell us that with Him there is no distinction between persons. There is no hierarchy. In God's Kingdom all are equal beloved children of the Father and there is no one greater than another. Love is there for all; as is grace. If only there was a way, even if just in our hearts, to eliminate the need to rank people; but to see everyone as a beloved person whether rich and successful or poor and in need–just as God sees us.

Prayer:

Heavenly Father, Thank You for loving us all despite rank or circumstance. Your grace is a gift we don't deserve and can't repay. That love brings rest and peace. Help us to remember that grace and extend it to others regardless of their status in society. **Amen**.

Hymn: "In Christ There Is No East or West" ELW 650

Acts 5:12-16

12 Now many signs and wonders were done among the people through the apostles. And they were all together in Solomon's Portico. **13** None of the rest dared to join them, but the people held them in high esteem. **14** Yet more than ever believers were added to the Lord, great numbers of both men and women, **15** so that they even carried out the sick into the streets and laid them on cots and mats, in order that Peter's shadow might fall on some of them as he came by. **16** A great number of people would also gather from the towns around Jerusalem, bringing the sick and those tormented by unclean spirits, and they were all cured.

***Poem:* to think of later**

I prefer to think of later
when we are in love
and we dance together
and mouth the words we cannot yet hear
because the music is so loud
we fall into each others arms
the moon shines bright enough
for us to cast shadows
and we laugh
at the tangle we make of our clothes
the sheets
our lives
the promise of forever

Meditation:

The Good News of Jesus Christ was spreading because of the work of the disciples following Jesus' death, resurrection, and ascension. According to Acts many men and women were touched by the love of God and the faith in His grace and healing ability. In our present day churches we continue this practice of faith and prayer for those in need of healing. We believe in the power of prayer and the work of God among the sick. God has blessed us greatly by inspiring advances in the medical field so that we have better health. God also has called individuals with specific gifts into work in the medical field. Just as God has called and uses pastors to spread the Word of the Gospel, God has called people with healing gifts to be doctors, nurses, therapists, lab research specialists, and more. Keep these called persons in your prayers as well to do the work for which God has called them as they assist God in healing our physical brokenness.

Prayer:

Healing Lord, we hold in prayers those who are sick and suffering; but also those whom You have called to care for them. Please bless the hands of those in the medical field with Your wisdom and abilities to heal alongside You. **Amen**.

Jude 1:17-25

17 But you, beloved, must remember the words previously spoken by the apostles of our Lord Jesus Christ, **18** for they said to you, "In the last time there will be scoffers, indulging their own ungodly lusts." **19** It is these worldly people, devoid of the Spirit, who are causing divisions. **20** But you, beloved, build yourselves up on your most holy faith; pray in the Holy Spirit; **21** keep yourselves in the love of God; look forward to the mercy of our Lord Jesus Christ that leads to eternal life. **22** And have mercy on some who are wavering; **23** save others by snatching them out of the fire; and have mercy on still others with fear, hating even the tunic defiled by their bodies.

Benediction

24 Now to him who is able to keep you from falling and to make you stand without blemish in the presence of his glory with rejoicing, **25** to the only God our Savior, through Jesus Christ our Lord, be glory, majesty, power, and authority, before all time and now and forever. Amen

Poem: **The Last Day**

The last day we visit each other
either me to you
or you to me
I will bake almond cookies
and let them get too dry
so we have to dip them in hot tea
longer than usual
until they are soft enough
that they dissolve on our tongues
and leave bits in the bottom of our cups

Meditation:

Our world is full of divisions from political to economic to recreational. Yes, recreational–just watch an American NFL football game or a College teams football game, especially in the South. We are divisive people who all think that our way is the right way and we are quick to criticize those whom we see as wrong. In this passage the writer is trying to get people to love and help one another, especially if it is across a division. Using the name of Christ the writer reminds us of mercy and love. Love that begs to be used to end divisions and build us all up as one together in Christ with mercy and grace at the core of how we treat one another; even on Super Bowl Sunday.

Prayer:

Lord God, help us to live in love with one another and give us a desire to end divisions. May we reach out to those in need and share our faith and strength. **Amen**.

Third Wednesday of Advent
December 17, 2025

Matthew 8:14-17
Matthew 8:28-34

14 When Jesus entered Peter's house, he saw his mother-in-law lying in bed with a fever; **15** he touched her hand, and the fever left her, and she got up and began to serve him. **16** That evening they brought to him many who were possessed by demons, and he cast out the spirits with a word and cured all who were sick. **17** This was to fulfill what had been spoken through the prophet Isaiah, "He took our infirmities and bore our diseases."

28 When he came to the other side, to the region of the Gadarenes, two men possessed by demons came out of the tombs and met him. They were so fierce that no one could pass that way. **29** Suddenly they shouted, "What have you to do with us, Son of God? Have you come here to torment us before the time?" **30** Now a large herd of swine was feeding at some distance from them. **31** The demons begged him, "If you cast us out, send us into the herd of swine." **32** And he said to them, "Go!" So they came out and entered the swine, and suddenly, the whole herd stampeded down the steep bank into the sea and drowned in the water. **33** The swineherds ran off, and, going into the town, they told the whole story about what had happened to the men possessed by demons. **34** Then the whole town came out to meet Jesus, and when they saw him they begged him to leave their region.

Poem: **A Frightening Hand**

It's ok to be afraid when you realize
the power the future will bring
despite all its promises of treasure
it moves with a frightening hand

I wish and I pray for salvation
for peace or for hope, or escape
but it terrorizes me to consider
what could drive my own demons away

a peal
a peal
from a tower
gracing the landscape
and as long as I've longed to hear it
I confess that it fill me with dread

Leave me now, I beg you
I've not understood what will be
and despite that we've come this long way
I'd rather dive into the sea

It's ok to be afraid in anticipation
of how you will retell this tale
rending beauty from the slop of my life
until my will no longer be done

Meditation:

When we read these stories of people tormented by demons we should pause to consider what that may symbolize in our own lives. What demons torment us? What do we carry around that causes us pain or to behave unlike ourselves? Prayer is a good place to start working through those demons. God is already with us; but it is good for us to take time to invite God in to help us heal from what hurts. God can help guide us to help and support as we struggle. God will bear the struggle with us. God knows that this world causes pain and God promises to never leave our side through it all.

Prayer:

Loving Lord, help and guide us when we are troubled. Walk with us to help us be free from our demons, whether they be addiction, sadness, grief, and so much more. Work in and through us to elevate love above all things that weigh us down. **Amen**.

Hymn: "Precious Lord, Take My Hand" ELW 773

December 18, 2025 – Thursday

Galatians 3:23-29

23 Now before faith came, we were imprisoned and guarded under the law until faith would be revealed. **24** Therefore the law was our disciplinarian until Christ came, so that we might be reckoned as righteous by faith. **25** But now that faith has come, we are no longer subject to a disciplinarian, **26** for in Christ Jesus you are all children of God through faith. **27** As many of you as were baptized into Christ have clothed yourselves with Christ. **28** There is no longer Jew or Greek; there is no longer slave or free; there is no longer male and female, for all of you are one in Christ Jesus. **29** And if you belong to Christ, then you are Abraham's offspring, heirs according to the promise.

Poem: **the duality of time**

The before and the after
we live in the duality of time
the world is like the pages of a book
we mark the center
always the center
between the unchangeable
the frozen
the said
the established
codified and inscribed
written before we are now
between the possibles
the fluid
the yet to be said
the fertile ground
yet to be sown

Meditation:

God's law gives us boundaries to try to live within; but like all laws divine or societal we can't seem to not cross those boundaries on a regular basis. Thankfully in Christ we experience incredible grace to fall, to make mistakes, to push the boundaries and still find a soft place to land. We are allowed to explore and make choices but there is always a forgiving place to come back to. God's arms are always reaching out to bring us all into a divine resting place of love and grace.

Prayer:

Lord God, thank You for Your embrace of love and grace, wrapping around our mistakes and law breaking habits. We are so used to negativity and consequences that unconditional love and grace is hard for us to understand. Thankfully we don't have to understand in order to rest in You. **Amen**.

December 19, 2025 – Friday

Galatians 4:1-7

4 My point is this: heirs, as long as they are minors, are no better than those who are enslaved, though they are the owners of all the property, **2** but they remain under guardians and trustees until the date set by the father. **3** So with us; while we were minors, we were enslaved to the elemental principles of the world. **4** But when the fullness of time had come, God sent his Son, born of a woman, born under the law, **5** in order to redeem those who were under the law, so that we might receive adoption as children. **6** And because you are children, God has sent the Spirit of his Son into our hearts, crying, "Abba! Father!" **7** So you are no longer a slave but a child, and if a child then also an heir through God.

Poem: of the beginning

children run and play
earthbound spirits
all possibility
but not truly free
unbound by certain destiny
always incarnating
the anticipation
of the beginning

Meditation:

Through baptism we all become a part of God's beloved family. There is nothing asked of us in order to receive that gift. We were all created by God because God decided the world needed someone like each of us. In baptism we are sealed with the Cross of Christ forever and given the power of the Holy Spirit to dwell within us. We are held as God's children both in this life and the eternal life to come. Take time to celebrate and remember that day of baptism and give thanks for the gift of love and adoption.

Prayer:

Heavenly Father, we thank You for creating us and adopting us into a family of love and light. Help us to practice grace and mercy within this family as we remember our baptisms and those of others. **Amen**.

John 3:31-36

31 The one who comes from above is above all; the one who is of the earth belongs to the earth and speaks about earthly things. The one who comes from heaven is above all. **32** He testifies to what he has seen and heard, yet no one accepts his testimony. **33** Whoever has accepted his testimony has certified this, that God is true. **34** He whom God has sent speaks the words of God, for he gives the Spirit without measure. **35** The Father loves the Son and has placed all things in his hands. **36** Whoever believes in the Son has eternal life; whoever disobeys the Son will not see life but must endure God's wrath.

Poem: **Speak to Me in Certainty**

Speak to me in certainty
speak to me in bold-faced text
and declaratives
I need a break
from this storm

But God also loves
the disobedient son
and the daughter who runs away
and those of us who hide ourselves
in loneliness and despair

Edict never speaks to me
Mere billboards yelling law
while I wrestle with quiet thoughts
fears and broken vows
disappointments I have caused

So speak to me in certainty
speak to me in shouts
new commandments you've distilled
through your own private bouts
but these, too, are earthly things

In anticipation of graces hand
and just maybe our own salvation
I await here trying not to think
of where this all might end
and I prepare for the beginning

Meditation:

God sent Jesus into our world to speak God's words to us; to remind us of the law but to teach us that love and grace are greater. We sit in excited anticipation at the end of this advent season to celebrate the birth of the Savior and to remember the enormity of God's love. Jesus taught us that God's words could be summed up by the command to love God and love our neighbors. In this life we strive to do both, falling short, but never giving up as the Spirit gives us strength to keep trying; as we cycle through a constant flow of grace and forgiveness.

Prayer:

Lord God, we are almost at the end of this advent of anticipation to celebrate Your incarnation and Your walk with us in our world. After the celebrations keep us mindful of the anticipation of the next time You come and our world is changed yet again by love. **Amen.**

Week 4:The Beginning

Fourth Sunday of Advent
December 21, 2025

Matthew 1:18-25

18 Now the birth of Jesus the Messiah took place in this way. When his mother Mary had been engaged to Joseph, but before they lived together, she was found to be pregnant from the Holy Spirit. **19** Her husband Joseph, being a righteous man and unwilling to expose her to public disgrace, planned to divorce her quietly. **20** But just when he had resolved to do this, an angel of the Lord appeared to him in a dream and said, "Joseph, son of David, do not be afraid to take Mary as your wife, for the child conceived in her is from the Holy Spirit. **21** She will bear a son, and you are to name him Jesus, for he will save his people from their sins." **22** All this took place to fulfill what had been spoken by the Lord through the prophet: **23** "Look, the virgin shall become pregnant and give birth to a son, and they shall name him Emmanuel," which means, "God is with us." **24** When Joseph awoke from sleep, he did as the angel of the Lord commanded him; he took her as his wife **25** but had no marital relations with her until she had given birth to a son, and he named him Jesus.

Poem: **The World Unfolds Before Us**

The world unfolds before us
in the most unremarkable way
and the poor just keep having babies

Troubles and doubts
beset each one of us who live
and we often choose the quiet way out

But it is in dreams that the truth is shown

So we put aside received indignities
that threaten to compromise our calm
and accept the impossible grace of it all

We speak our truth to no one
convinced this is the way
and raise our children as they are
But it is in dreams that the truth is shown

We arise each and every morning
we face each difficult day
and we are patient with our unfulfilled desire

Though we know that God is with us
we maybe give it another name
And play the hand we're dealt

But it is in dreams that the truth is shown

Meditation:

We know the story and we love it. We love to tell it each year as we remember what we have created in our minds and hearts of what that silent night looked like–the peace and hope that the promise creates. I can't help but think of how heavy Joseph and Mary must have felt under the weight of this responsibility. I also am in awe of their faith and trust in God's plan. Would I be willing to risk everything in that way? I'm not sure; but I'm grateful that they were. I'm grateful for the enormity of God's love to come and walk among us beginning as a baby in a manger.

Prayer:

God of grace and love, we give You thanks and praise for the gift of Your presence in Christ Jesus, our Savior born through extraordinary circumstances into a hurting world, and the Holy Spirit that continues to work and dwell among us. Be with us as our anticipation becomes celebration. **Amen**.

Hymn: "O Come, O Come, Emmanuel" ELW 257

About the Authors:

Rev. Jamie Witt is an ordained pastor in the ELCA (Evangelical Lutheran Church in America) who joyfully serves the beloved congregation at Lutheran Church of the Good Shepherd in Douglasville, Georgia. She received her M.Div. degree from Luther Seminary in Minneapolis/St. Paul. She currently lives with her daughter, Anna, and their 3 dogs and 2 cats in a small town in Georgia. In her spare time she enjoys reading mystery novels, crocheting, music, and mostly spending time with loved ones (which includes the dogs and cats).

Kevin Schumaker is an attorney, poet, and performer who desperately tries to be joyful, but often settles for mildly annoyed. When not practicing criminal defense across the Atlanta metro area he reads, plays video games, and feeds his spoiled lab Mollie too many treats. He is married with one amazing daughter. His previous works include **That'll Leave a Mark**, a collection of poetry in the beat and existentialist traditions. The follow-up, **An Even Bigger Mark**, is anticipated for a 2026 release.

peace be with you